Clarinet

Level 2–3

Alfred's
INSTRUMENTAL
PLAY-ALONG

Top Praise & Worship Instrumental Solos

MW01153008

CONTENTS

*Download free MP3 Demo and Play-Along tracks at www.alfred.com.
Simply enter product number 34225 into the search window to locate the book and corresponding recordings.

Arranged by Bill Galliford, Ethan Neuburg and Tod Edmondson

© 2009 Alfred Music Publishing Co., Inc.
All Rights Reserved. Printed in USA.

ISBN-10: 0-7390-6592-0
ISBN-13: 978-0-7390-6592-1

Alfred

Track 2: Demo
Track 3: Play Along

EVERLASTING GOD

Words and Music by
BRENTON BROWN and KEN RILEY

Everlasting God - 2 - 1
34225

BEAUTIFUL ONE

Track 4: Demo
Track 5: Play Along

Words and Music by
TIM HUGHES

BLESSED BE YOUR NAME

Track 6: Demo
Track 7: Play Along

Words and Music by
BETH REDMAN and MATT REDMAN

GOD OF WONDERS

Track 8: Demo
Track 9: Play Along

Words and Music by
MARC BYRD and STEVE HINDALONG

THE WONDERFUL CROSS

Track 10: Demo
Track 11: Play Along

Words and Music by
CHRIS TOMLIN, J.D. WALT
and JESSE REEVES

Moderate rock (♩ = 92) *Verse:*

34225

HERE I AM TO WORSHIP
(LIGHT OF THE WORLD)

Words and Music by
TIM HUGHES

YOU ARE MY ALL IN ALL

Track 14: Demo
Track 15: Play Along

Words and Music by
DENNIS JERNIGAN

HOLY IS THE LORD

Words and Music by
CHRIS TOMLIN and LOUIE GIGLIO

Track 18: Demo
Track 19: Play Along

HOW GREAT IS OUR GOD

Words and Music by
CHRIS TOMLIN, ED CASH
and JESSE REEVES

Chorus:

INDESCRIBABLE

Track 20: Demo
Track 21: Play Along

Words and Music by
JESSE REEVES and LAURA STORY

Indescribable - 2 - 2
34225

JESUS MESSIAH

Track 22: Demo
Track 23: Play Along

Words and Music by
DANIEL CARSON, CHRIS TOMLIN,
ED CASH and JESSE REEVES

Moderately slow (♩ = 84)

Jesus Messiah - 2 - 1
34225

LORD I LIFT YOUR NAME ON HIGH

Free MP3 download*

Words and Music by
RICK FOUNDS

Latin, salsa style (♩ = 96)

Lord I Lift Your Name on High - 2 - 1
34225

Download free MP3 Demo and Play-Along tracks at www.alfred.com. Simply enter product number 34225 into the search window to locate the book and corresponding recordings.

MARVELOUS LIGHT

Words and Music by
CHARLIE HALL

PARTS OF A CLARINET AND FINGERING CHART

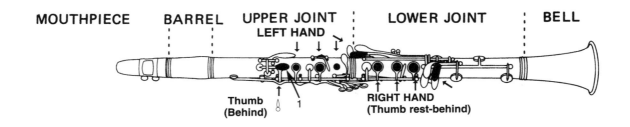

● = press the key or cover the hole with your finger.
○ = do not press the key or cover the hole.

When there is more than one fingering given for a note, use the first one unless the alternate fingering is suggested.

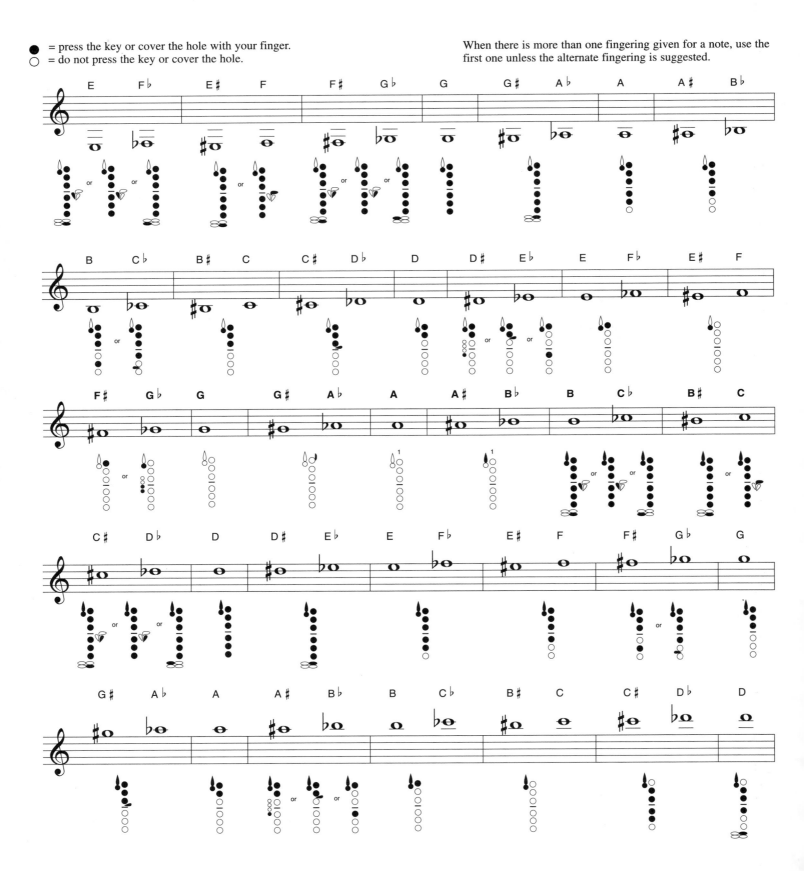